40

Days

At The

WELL

Jeffrey A. Wilson

6:3
Ministries

ISBN: 978-0-615-92334-5

6:3 Ministries
Jackson, MO 63755

www.6-3ministries.org

DEDICATION

First, and foremost, to God. He is the one that gives the inspiration and passion for His Word. To my beloved Julee. Without her urging I never would have dreamed I could accomplish this. I love you. 6:3. And to my grandpa (Pa Pa) who believed enough in my calling to let me preach my first sermon, under his ministry, at 15 years old. You get to share in this ministry.

CONTENTS

ACKNOWLEDGMENTS

Thank you to all my family and friends who supported me over the past two and a half years. You walked through life with me. Thank you. And to my good friends and editors, Larry Shafer, Crystal Shafer, and Jennifer Crass I owe my deepest appreciation. Your suggestions and critique helped make this the best it could be.

INTRODUCTION

Imagine what it must have been like for the disciples to sit at Jesus' feet. They could hear Him. They could touch Him. They could ask Him questions. Oh, how I wish that could have been me! While He may not physically be here we know that's only one part of creation. Jesus still shares with us through His Word, the Bible. This is where this book starts.

In October, 2012, God began dealing with me to share my thoughts with a 'broader audience'. I didn't fully understand what He meant at the time. Slowly but surely He started revealing to me what He was doing. That's when I started a blog. Initially I thought it would be a place to 'scratch the ministry itch' while I waited for His direction for 'real ministry'. Little did I know that this was the real ministry that He had in mind. As of September, 2013 – less than one year later – *Drawing from the Well* has been read in almost 40 countries across the globe. This book is a 40 day journey through those writings.

So even though we can't see or touch Jesus, He is still speaking. I invite you to sit at the well with me and draw deeply. After all "...whoever drinks the water I [Jesus] give them will never thirst... (John 4:14)"

DAY 1

I like cartoons. I know…it's a statement that you probably didn't expect to hear from 'someone my age'. But I really do. I find that they can be entertaining, funny, and instructional all at the same time. Where else can you learn how not to construct Road Runner traps? I don't watch cartoons for that reason though. Normally it's to check out from reality for a little bit. After all…nowhere in history do we ever see Teenage Mutant Ninja Turtles.

There's a scene in Disney's *Cars 2* that has earned a permanent place in my memory. It's the one where Mater is getting a holographic disguise for his 'assignment'. The computer probes, measures, and scans and finally projects a perfect disguise — well almost. There are some issues. Mater has some dents and dings that the computer can't cope with. The disguise doesn't quite 'fit'. When asked to fix the dents, Mater responds that he doesn't want them fixed, buffed, filled, or anything else. He values them too much. Really? He values the dents? He then says that each one of them occurred when he was with his best friend, Lightning McQueen, and he wanted to remember them forever. Of course…when I heard that I immediately knew where God was going to take that one.

Our life can seem like it has lots of dents. A turmoil here, a crisis there. Pretty soon we look like we're rusted and dented. Seeing our self in the mirror we think that all of those scars, dings, and dents need to be fixed before we're ready for God to work through us. What we don't realize, though, is that God was working in us the whole time life was beating up on us. Life has done its share of beating up on me. It has left numerous scars and dents. But, just like Mater, I don't want them fixed. Each of them has provided invaluable lessons to use in touching the lives of others. Without those dents, I wouldn't remember the grace and mercy of God in the same way. When others tell me how life is beating them up, I couldn't speak to persevering through trials if the dents weren't there.

When the Israelites finally moved in to take the Promised Land Joshua commanded one person from each tribe to place a stone in the middle of the Jordan River. These stones were to be a reminder to them for generations as to what God did for His people. The dents serve that purpose in us. These things aren't scars that point to life's cruelty. They're trophies that testify to God's goodness. The dents proclaim God's mercy and faithfulness. They remind us of His promises to always walk through life with us (Isaiah 43:2). They teach us that, although we must suffer some in this life, God is always there to bring us through it (1 Peter 5:10). They comfort us with the realization that we're never alone (Deuteronomy 31:8). So why would we want them to be fixed? Removing the dents removes the reminders.

Life hurts sometimes — a lot of the time, if we're honest. When it beats us up and leaves dings and dents we need to take on Mater's attitude. When asked about the dents our response needs to be, "I come by each one of 'em with my best friend Jesus Christ. I don't fix these. I wanna remember these dents forever."

DAY 2

1. You're in good hands.

2. Have it your way.

3. It keeps going and going and going.

4. Melts in your mouth, not in your hands.

5. Obey your thirst.

6. So easy a caveman can do it.

7. I'm lovin' it.

8. Think outside the bun.

9. Just do it.

10. Can you hear me now?

Can you name those companies? You probably can and then some. So why am I talking about advertising slogans? Because they all compete to be the one thing that we purchase or rely on to fill a need. They're all around us and are constantly changing. New companies will pop up to compete with 'the big boys'. Old rivals will update their advertising to draw the market focus back to them. Advertising is a billion dollar industry. Just look at the amount of money spent for a 30 second advertisement during the Super Bowl. It's a staggering number.

All these companies have one thing in common. They're all trying to get us to trust their product. That's a difficult thing to do in the world we live in. The internet and social media have made it possible for anyone to advertise to thousands upon thousands of people instantly. New and innovative ways of spreading the word about products and services abound. All vying for our focus, attention, and consumption.

As you read this you may be wondering what the spiritual implication of this is. Is there a correlation between modern-day advertising and the Bible? Why yes, yes there is. It is this. The biggest advertisements available don't detail any company's accomplishments or product. They detail the glory of God.

Everywhere we look we see ads for God and His glory. The splendor of Niagara Falls or the Grand Canyon. The majesty of the Milky Way or the brilliance of the full moon. The beauty of a sunrise or sunset. The relief of a spring rain. The stillness of new fallen snow. Every one of these things are seen day after day, month after month, season after season, and year after year. They have not changed to garner the attention of new generations. They have not been tweaked to reach a certain demographic. They are not updated with new graphics or music. Just like God…they are there. Always the same, always reminding us of the glory of our Creator.

Every morning just before I get to work I have the privilege of seeing one of these advertisements. To my right I get to see the sun crest the horizon as it greets a new day. Each time I see it I am reminded of what David wrote, "The heavens declare the glory of God; the skies proclaim the work of his hands. (Psalm 19:1)" It is breathtaking and wondrous to behold. The writer of Ecclesiastes put it this way, "Truly the light is sweet, And it is pleasant for the eyes to behold the sun; (Ecclesiastes 11:7)" Paul said this to the Corinthians, "The sun has one kind of splendor, the moon another and the stars another; and star differs from star in splendor. (1 Corinthians 15:41)"

In the movie, Men In Black, there is a line that caught my attention. Tommy Lee Jones' character looks up to the starry sky and reminisces about how beautiful they are. He never looks at them but starts to realize how breathtaking each one is. In this world of billboards, internet ads, commercials, and slogans I have a challenge for you. Look at the advertisements of God. See the splendor and majesty of the One Who made it all. Then, like David, "…see that the Lord is good…(Psalm 34:8)"

DAY 3

"**G**o ahead, treat yourself. You deserve it!" We've heard — and probably said — that phrase more times than we can count. And there are times that it is appropriate. Something we said, did, or endured earned us the right to whatever it was we wanted. As I thought about that phrase, though, my mind turned (as it most often does) to the spiritual side of things.

In reality I was thinking about this generation of kids. Having two myself and being the stepparent of one (making it 3 in our house at times) makes things interesting. To be quite honest, there seems to be a sense of entitlement or deserving things regardless of attitudes or actions. It would be funny if it wasn't so frustrating at times. "No" has become a regular part of my vocabulary...but I digress. There really is a point to this...I promise.

As the kids (and their attitude of deserving) rolled around on my mind I began to compare it to my own attitudes toward God. What I realized is that I really don't get from Him what I deserve. I feel like I do so well until I begin to realize that, many times, the things I do are part of my checklist. I pat myself on the back because I'm doing such a great job and then wonder why God isn't beaming about the things I do.

The book of Job starts out in an interesting way. "…Have you considered my servant Job? There is no one on earth like him; he is blameless and upright, a man who fears God and shuns evil. (Job 1:8)" God says that Job is an upstanding guy. A man who ran from evil. I really think it is more than that though. I believe that his heart was right before God. Here's why. We know that God is the same…that He never changes (Hebrews 13:8). We also know that through His word He judges the thoughts and actions of the heart (Hebrews 4:12). Because of these things God wasn't looking at Job's actions but at his heart. And Job was right in his heart.

All too often we get upset at God because He doesn't give us what we think we deserve. But have we stopped and considered the motivation behind wanting those things? Are we acting like our kids and thinking that it is God's job to take care of us…so we should get everything we want? Or have we understood that we deserve nothing because of our sin…our failure to love God with all of our heart. And it is in our heart that we feel like we either deserve something from God or we want to give something to God.

I don't know about you…but I really don't want God to give me what I deserve. I want to say what David did, "Create in me a pure heart, O God, and renew a steadfast spirit within me. (Psalm 51:10)" So my prayer would go something like this…

God, forgive me for the times that I got upset because I didn't get what I thought I deserved. I know that Your grace and mercy give me more than I ever really do deserve. Purify my heart, mind, and motivations so that they really do please You. Thank You for all the unseen blessings that you give me every day. And may I be deserving of your grace through your Son, Jesus.

DAY 4

A couple of weeks ago my men's life group leader assigned some 'homework'. He had been thinking about the verse in Galatians 5 that lists the fruit of the Spirit. Over the next few days as I drove home from work (a 45 minute commute) my normal list of podcasts began taking on a theme. In particular one of my regular listening broadcasts. T D Jakes was sharing a series titled The Love Letter. He made the following statement in his message 'Love has no Loopholes', "If He commands me to do it…then it must be in my power to accomplish it. That means love is controllable." And something clicked.

To really understand what clicked you need a little background. When asked what the greatest commandment was Jesus gave two. "Jesus replied: 'Love the Lord your God with all your heart and with all your soul and with all your mind.' This is the first and greatest commandment. And the second is like it: 'Love your neighbor as yourself.' (Matthew 22:37-39)"

Most of us have heard and/or quoted these verses but this time it was different. I asked God to reveal something new about this and how it relates to the fruit of the Spirit. And then I started listening. Here's what I believe He began to (and continues to) show me.

We tend to think about love as an emotion. We think of it in terms of feelings for our children, parents, friends, family, and others. How we feel about the person determines the level of love we have for them. But that's not what Jesus is saying. He says it is a commandment. He says it is something we HAVE to do. In fact…it's the biggest thing that we have to do.

In addition to the degrees of love that we feel for people, we think it can change based on circumstances or something another person does to us. For example…the husband or wife files for divorce stating, "I just don't love you anymore." The kids say that they don't love their parents because they won't get them the latest thing that they want. It's all event-driven. We love…based on how we…FEEL.

But what if love isn't a feeling at all? No…I'm not talking about Boston's song, "More Than a Feeling" or the cliché statements like, "Love is an action." What if our capacity to love is based on choosing to offer grace and mercy even when we don't feel like it? Does that sound familiar? It should. That's what Jesus did for us.

Let's go a little bit deeper into this. The first item mentioned in the list of the fruit of the Spirit is LOVE. It's not something that is *given* to us. We don't *learn* to love…we *choose* to love. We decide whether we will follow God's commandment or whether we will break it. It's totally up to us.

So the next time I say the words, "I love you" to my wife they will carry a different meaning. I'm not saying that I feel something (although I definitely do). It's a decision on my part to follow the commandment of the Almighty. I am making a choice to follow in the footsteps of Jesus and love regardless of what is returned. Let's face it…if we all did more of that the world we live in would be a very different place.

DAY 5

Trouble can come in many shapes and sizes. It rears its head in the form of a layoff or pay freeze. It shows up as an illness or broken down car. It appears as a rumor that threatens to destroy relationships. Regardless of how it is manifest one thing holds true — no one likes trouble.

The sad fact of reality is that we will all have trouble. In some way, it will put its mark on all of us at one time or another (probably multiple times in our lives). And that can be a depressing thought. But if we look at just the trouble then we discount all of the things that the trouble can do for us. Of all the things that teach us in life…none is as good at teaching as trouble. It teaches us how strong we are (and you are stronger than you think). It reveals character. It does so many things that we can miss if we were to escape it.

I believe that all too often we ask God to take us out of the trouble we are in because it seems so unbearable at the time. We tend to have such a narrow focus because all we see is the pain of the trial. Because of the narrow focus (understandably so at the time) we think that we're going through it alone. But there's so many promises that show us that we're not alone even in the trouble.

There's not one place in Scripture that I can find where we're alone in our trouble. There are, however, multiple places where it is stated that we're not alone. Here's just a few…

- "…He will never leave you nor forsake you…(Deuteronomy 31:6, 8)"
- "I will not leave you as orphans; I will come to you. (John 14:18)"
- "I have told you these things, so that in me you may have peace. In this world you will have trouble. But take heart! I have overcome the world. (John 16:33)"

But though I see these verses…it doesn't make it any easier when I'm in the middle of trouble, does it? The answer to that is a resounding, "NO!" And I'm sure that everyone can relate. What about when we're in the middle of things? Is there something that we can cling to that will give us hope in the troubled times? That answer is a resounding, "YES!" God never *puts us in something*…He *takes us through it*. While there are promises that He doesn't leave us…there are more that say He's walking through it with us.

David walked through some dark times. He understood this principle and wrote about it in Psalm 23:4. "Even though I walk through the darkest valley, I will fear no evil, for you are with me; your rod and your staff, they comfort me." This is a picture of the shepherd guiding the sheep through a dark valley. There can be no guidance without the shepherd walking through the valley with the sheep. The truth in this is that God doesn't send us in alone. He walks through the trouble WITH us. Look at Isaiah 43:2, "When you pass **through** the waters, I will be with you; and when you pass **through** the rivers, they will not sweep over you. When you walk **through** the fire, you will not be burned; the flames will not set you ablaze." There's a dual promise here. The first is that we will get through it. The trial will not destroy us. The second is that we're not alone in the middle of it. God promises to walk through the trouble with us. So go ahead trouble…bring it on! While it's not easy it will not destroy me. For I know that it only deepens my trust in the God who never leaves me in the middle.

DAY 6

There's a story in Mark (Mark 9:14-24 to be exact) about Jesus delivering a boy from a demon possession. The thing that intrigues me about this passage is the conversation that the boy's father and Jesus have. He asks some clarifying questions and then this conversation takes place:

"It has often thrown him into fire or water to kill him. But if you can do anything, take pity on us and help us." "'If you can'?" said Jesus. "Everything is possible for one who believes." Immediately the boy's father exclaimed, "I do believe; help me overcome my unbelief! (Mark 9:22-24)"

This had been going on for quite a while. It sounds like, from the context, that the father was running out of hope that it would ever be fixed. Hmmm…that sounds familiar. Something happens that goes on and on and on. There's no light at the end of the tunnel…no hope of being corrected. Frustration and disappointment are around every corner as the situation is dealt with.

But then Jesus steps in and hope stirs. The father desperately pleads with Jesus that if He can do anything...please help. There are a couple of things to note in this passage.

1. Jesus senses the hopelessness. "'If you can'?" said Jesus. "Everything is possible for one who believes. (Mark 9:23)". We come to Jesus just like this don't we? We plead for relief from the situation in a desperate hope that there will be a breakthrough, or something will change. Jesus senses it every time and His response is always the same...just believe. That seems like a simple statement although we all know it isn't that easy. Believing means not looking at the facts. It means not seeing that there's no more money left to pay the overdue bills. It means not looking at the duct tape and bubble gum that holds the car together. That's not an easy thing to do.

2. The father acknowledges his unbelief. "Immediately the boy's father exclaimed, "I do believe; help me overcome my unbelief! (Mark 9:24)" If we are honest with ourselves we will see that this is all too common in us. We see most clearly in the physical. We see the overdue mortgage in front of us. We see the sick child in front of us. We see the empty pantry in front of us. It stares us in the face, mocking, taunting, saying that nothing can be done. Then we feel hope stirring. Jesus has stepped in and we want to believe...but...there's all this stuff staring us in the face. So what do we do?

I believe that the best thing that we can do is just what this father did. Realize that we are only human and we sometimes worry. But that worry can't overtake the confidence that trust in Jesus gives us. He never goes back on his promises. One of those promises is this..."And my God will meet all your needs according to the riches of his glory in Christ Jesus. (Philippians 4:19)" The question becomes this…will you still believe? Will you understand that there is a part of you that doesn't see a way out? Will you go against what you see and trust in Jesus that He will supply your need? This father did and his son was delivered.

DAY 7

I've been thinking a lot about the past lately. As I think about recent past events I am reminded of a favorite verse of mine. It reads, "Forget the former things; do not dwell on the past. (Isaiah 43:18)" This is a tough verse to live up to.

The human brain has a remarkable ability to recall details of past events with such great clarity sometimes. I say 'sometimes' because, most of the time, the details can be cloudy. Our perception is usually obscured by the emotions that we felt at the time of the event that we are recalling. If it's a happy event we feel all warm and fuzzy. If it's a sad or angry event…well, we feel just the opposite of that. And that's the problem with holding onto past events.

You see…holding onto those events anchors us to that point in life. We all know the function of an anchor. Its sole purpose is to keep the ship from moving from the spot it is currently in. When we hold onto a past event we keep our life from moving in the direction that God is trying to get us to go. We essentially keep ourselves from living life because we're stuck holding onto something that does us no good. Israel did that with Egypt and it got them into _huge_ trouble.

Another thing that holding onto past events does is keep us from seeing future opportunities. We tend to filter things in life through the emotions of the event or circumstance. When we do that our perception is skewed and, therefore, so is our reality. Opportunities to grow and learn are missed because of this unrealistic view of life and all that it holds.

Yet another thing that this can do is drain us of hope. When we anchor our self to these circumstances and filter life's outlook through it we tend to live a hopeless, joyless life. Our trust and joy is shattered almost beyond repair as we perceive that life will just hand us another hurt, pain, or hardship. So what do we do about it? Is there hope for us? I believe there is.

We cannot change the past. We can only learn from it and allow those lessons to affect the present and our future. The verse that you read above is only the first half of a statement that God is making. Isaiah 43:19 reads, "See, I am doing a new thing! Now it springs up; do you not perceive it? I am making a way in the wilderness and streams in the wasteland." Now that's what I'm talking about!! God tells us to forget the former things because He is doing something new. That's what we need to look for. That's what we need to hope for. Every night ends and a new day dawns. God wants us to forget the former things, not so we fail to learn from the past, but so that we don't live in it. We can only see the new things if we're looking for them and the way to do that is to "...fix our eyes on Jesus...(Hebrews 2:12)"

DAY 8

"Don't pray for patience. If you do…God will send trials your way." I have heard this mentioned so many times that I've lost count. And every time I hear it I sort of chuckle. Because God is going to send trials into our life. It's just a part of life with God. It's how we deal with the impending trials that make us or break us.

"Consider it pure joy, my brothers and sisters, whenever you face trials of many kinds, because you know that the testing of your faith produces perseverance. Let perseverance finish its work so that you may be mature and complete, not lacking anything. (James 1:2-4)" In the King James Version the word patience is used. Actually they are interchangeable here. The word from which we get patience or perseverance means "a patient enduring, sustaining, perseverance." And isn't this what we really want? We want to persevere…to go through it and come out shining for His glory on the other side. The problem comes when we want to skip the lessons and go straight to the blessing.

Recently my daughter went on a summer field trip. It was to a pottery shop. It's a place where they get to choose a particular item and paint and decorate it. Then the shop finishes the item and you get it back in a few days (about 2 weeks). The finishing process is like any other pottery item. It has to be fired. Heat is applied so that the item is strengthened for use. Without this process finishing the item would be so fragile that it couldn't be used. If we skip the finishing process we will be missing important things in our lives that strengthen and sustain us for God's use.

"But they're so hard to take." I agree. It's never easy to go through the trials. Pain hurts. But while we have to go through them...we're never alone in the midst of them. God promises that He will walk through them with us. I read a story one day that may illustrate this a little better...

"Some time ago, a few ladies met in a certain city to study the scriptures. While reading the third chapter of Malachi, they came up-on a remarkable expression in the third verse:

'And He shall sit as a refiner and purifier of silver (Malachi 3:3)'

One lady proposed to visit a silversmith, and report to them on what he said about the subject. She went accordingly, and without telling the object of her errand, begged the silversmith to tell her about the process of refining silver. After he had fully described it to her, she asked, 'But Sir, do you sit while the work of refining is going on?'

'Oh, yes madam,' replied the silversmith; 'I must sit with my eyes steadily fixed on the furnace, for if the time necessary for refining be exceeded in the slightest degree, the silver will be injured.'

The lady at once saw the beauty, and comfort too, of the expression, 'He shall sit as a refiner and purifier of silver.' God sees it needful to put His children into a furnace; His eye is steadily intent on the work of purifying, and His wisdom and love are both engaged in the best manner for us. Our trials do not come at random, and He will not let us be tested beyond what we can endure.

Before she left, the lady asked one final question, 'When do you know the process is complete?'

'Why, that is quite simple,' replied the silversmith. 'When I can see my own image in the silver, the refining process is finished.'" (Author Unknown)

While it's tempting to avoid the trials…doing so will only produce a life that is fragile and unfit for use. But if we embrace the trials that come our way we will be "…mature and complete, not lacking anything." In other words — a life that reflects the character of God.

DAY 9

Desperate times call for desperate measures. Most of us have heard that saying before. It is true. In desperate times people do things they wouldn't normally do. It's a place where all bets are off and nothing matters other than finding a solution to the issue at hand. And nothing will keep you from finding that solution.

Webster's dictionary defines desperate as, "involving or employing extreme measures in an attempt to escape defeat or frustration." I believe it's safe to say that much of the church today lives in a state of frustration. I am convinced that one of the reasons that the church (and Christians) in America do not see God moving like we want Him to is that we're not desperate enough. We live our lives in frustration feeling like that's all there is. We have bought the lie that life will never change and this is how it will be so we may as well live with it. Nothing could be further from the truth!

A friend of mine posted the following quote by Dan Henderson and Jim Cymbala at the Praying Church Conference in Cartersville,

Georgia. "Effective prayer ministry and life is always birthed through desperation." It seems to me that we should live in a state of desperation for God's power to move in and through us.

When you're desperate nothing will hold you back from the goal. There's nothing more to lose. You're desperate. And God loves it when we get to that place. He loves it when we're desperate because we'll do anything. And He's in the business of doing anything.

When you're desperate…you'll look anywhere and everywhere for a way out. (You will seek me and find me when you seek me with all your heart. Jeremiah 29:13)

When you're desperate…fear goes out the window. (For God has not given us a spirit of fear and timidity, but of power, love, and self-discipline. 2 Timothy 1:7)

When you're desperate…you'll try anything, and listen to anyone with an answer. (Now to him who is able to do immeasurably more than all we ask or imagine, according to his power that is at work within us, Ephesians 3:20)

Nothing is off-limits when you're desperate. And God looks for desperate hearts to work through. He worked in a desperate teenage boy and used him to kill a giant. He worked in a desperate woman and, through her, birthed one of the greatest prophets in the Old Testament (Samuel). God loves desperation because it reveals our weakness. "That is why, for Christ's sake, I delight in weaknesses, in insults, in hardships, in persecutions, in difficulties. For when I am weak, then I am strong. (2 Corinthians 12:10)"

So we need to ask ourselves a question. "How desperate are we?"

Do we see life as a revolving door with no hope of anything ever changing? Or are we desperate enough for change that we will do anything? Desperate times call for desperate measures. Maybe, just maybe, if we allow God to start working we will see the change that we so desperately want to see.

DAY 10

We have all experienced tests of our faith at one time or another. While they are not pleasant things James tells us to, "Consider it pure joy…" when they come (James 1:2). But that's not what this is about. Sometimes we attribute a trial or circumstance to having our faith tested when that's not the case. I know, I know…you're thinking, "Then what is it?" Well, I'm glad that you asked.

About 4 years ago I was driving to work and my mind was pondering some 'stuff' that was going on. What it was is not relevant…but let's just say that it wasn't pleasant. As my mind churned — trying to find a solution to these things — God spoke something to my heart. He said, "Sometimes I don't walk you through something to test you. Sometimes I do it to prove to you who I am." Wow! What a revelation!

I had the privilege to live 2 hours from Disneyland when my children were smaller. This was a great thing because one year for Christmas we got season passes (the good ones…with no blackout dates). We could plan trips to the theme park. But we could also just decide to get up and go for the day. Now it's hard to describe Disneyland to someone who hasn't been there. They can read about it and hear about it but it's not the same as being there. They don't understand the wonder of seeing the park and walking down Main Street. They have only seen pictures of Cinderella's castle. But if you've been there it's different. You can describe it in ways that only experience will allow.

What does this have to do with God revealing Himself? Well...

- If you've never been sick...God couldn't prove to you that He's your **Healer**.

- If you've never had a financial need...God couldn't prove to you that He's your **Provider**.

- If you've never been in trouble...God couldn't prove to you that He's your **Deliverer**.

- If you've never been worried...God couldn't prove to you that He's your **Peace**.

We're too quick to assume that all difficult circumstances are tests of faith and we immediately ask, "Why am I going through this?" And when we don't get the answer that we think we need we assume that God isn't listening. But what if we're asking the wrong question? Instead of asking why...maybe we need to ask, "What are you trying to reveal to me, Lord? Who are you in this?" These questions open us up to new revelations of who He is. And those revelations give us a picture of God that only experience will allow. It draws us closer and closer to Him.

Tests of faith will come. They're inevitable. But sometimes the things that we think are tests are in fact opportunities for God to reveal Himself to us in deeper ways. They're chances for us to experience the things of God that we read about in His Word. So...don't be afraid to ask, "What are you trying to reveal to me, God?" Then be ready for an answer that will blow your mind.

DAY 11

"Keep me as the apple of your eye; hide me in the shadow of your wings. (Psalm 17:8)" As I thought about this verse the last half just really stuck with me. "...hide me in the shadow of your wings." What a picture of God's protection!

Not long ago my wife and I were driving to a church service in another town. As we traveled along the rural highway that is so common in Southeast Missouri we rounded a corner to see a raccoon crossing the road. This in itself was a surprise to me as I'm from the California coast and don't see many raccoons. But even more interesting was that it was a mother raccoon and her three small babies. And they were all crossing the road in a nice, neat line. That is until we came around the corner. In an instant the mother was shielding her children from the looming danger that was barreling toward them. (For those of you that are wondering...I was able to slow down and go around them safely so mother raccoon and babies were all safe).

That's just what David is talking about in this verse. He is asking God for this type of protection. He is asking God to step between him and the looming danger that is right on top of Him. And the thing is that God loves to do just that. David knew this…because he knew God.

So what does it mean for us? It means exactly the same thing. While we may not have the same enemies that David did…we still have enemies. He is known as "the accuser of the brethren", or "Satan", or "the devil" and is constantly on the lookout for ways to attack us (1 Peter 5:8). If that was the end of the story it would be depressing. But it's not the end!

We can say the same thing that David said — "…hide me in the shadow of your wings." It's a call for God to step in between you and the raging storm that threatens to destroy you. It's a call for God to swoop in and rescue from certain doom as the circumstances of life overwhelm you. It's a call for God to rescue you from the enemies that prowl and attack.

But can we really know that God will be there when we call? Absolutely!

- "When I called, you answered me…(Psalm 138:3)."
- "You came near when I called you, and you said, 'Do not fear.' (Lamentations 3:57)"
- "I call on you, my God, for you will answer me…(Psalm 17:6)"

We can call on God as the storm rages and danger charges and have the confidence that God will hide us in the shadow of His wings. His protection will overshadow us and we can be confident that we'll be ok.

DAY 12

"Do not despise these small beginnings, for the Lord rejoices to see the work begin, to see the plumb line in Zerubbabel's hand. (Zechariah 4:10 — NLT)" Something has been turning over and over in my mind. It's just a thought...but as I pondered it I could see something growing. Nothing starts out huge. Even the tallest buildings in the world were started with a shovel. They didn't start big...they started with something small. All things in life have the smallest thing in common. Life starts with a small, single cell. Clothes start out with a single thread.

The phrase "small things" or "small beginnings" in this verse means young, small, insignificant, unimportant. We tend to dismiss small things. They're insignificant and unimportant. These small things, though, tend to play very important roles. The largest automobiles fail to start without the correct key...and it's small enough to fit in a pocket. The world's largest aircraft are held together with small screws and bolts. Some of the worst diseases known to man are caused by organisms that can only be seen through a microscope. Small things are NOT insignificant.

We are confronted with big, huge, massive issues each and every day. It's part of life on this planet. But that doesn't mean that small things can't make a difference.

- Goliath was killed by a small teenage boy.
- Jesus fed about 25,000 people with 5 rolls and 2 fish.
- Naaman was cured of leprosy because a small slave girl spoke up.

We need not dismiss the small things in our own lives as insignificant either. The smallest things said, or a smile given can make all the difference in the life of someone else. An encouraging word in the midst of a stressful situation can brighten the days ahead for the struggling person. These things may be small...but they are not insignificant. They are important. They are vital. They can make all the difference in the lives of those they touch.

What we must understand about these small things is that they get bigger. A seed, when watered, grows and has the potential to touch the sky. In the same way, a smile, encouraging word, or act of kindness has the potential to grow into something huge in the life of the person receiving it. And we get to have a hand in that person's touch from God.

So the next time you see something small...take another look. The next time we think the smile or encouraging word won't make a difference...think again. It may just be that the small thing we dismiss is the huge thing they needed to overcome something difficult in their life. We get to be the instrument of delivery used in God's hand.

DAY 13

I have been thinking about the promises of God over the last little while and each time another one comes to mind I just have to smile. Having grown up in church I heard a lot about God's promises. But after experiencing some of them first hand I must admit that my perspective on them has changed.

In American culture a promise is something that is used and, many times, viewed lightly. Our kids use it to get out of trouble. "I PROMISE I'll be good." We as parents use it to appease our children. "I PROMISE I'll play after my nap." Companies and corporations make promises to their customers to assure them of a certain level of service. All of these things happen every day without us thinking about it.

Paul wrote to the Corinthian church about this subject when he said, "For no matter how many promises God has made, they are "Yes" in Christ...(2 Corinthians 1:20)" My pastor has been preaching a series on Sunday mornings entitled 'Pleasing God'. He talked one week about the essential element in pleasing God...faith. As I thought about God's promises to me (specific ones) and the ones to His people I came back to this essential element. You see if we say that we love and believe God…then that means we believe that His promises are true. And if we believe the promises are true…then we should expect them to be fulfilled in us.

Could it be that our culture has had an effect on our belief in the promises of God? Doesn't God promise things to us in His Word? Shouldn't we trust God enough that He will keep the things He says? Why then do we not see more of Him working and fulfilling those promises in our lives? If we look in the mirror I believe we will find the answer to that question.

The good news though is that we can change how and when these promises are placed into our lives. You see…all it takes is a little exercise. We need to exercise our faith in God. God says that He doesn't show favoritism. We know what that is…right? It means preferential treatment. The misconception is that we have to attain a certain status before God will deliver on His promises to us. But that's contrary to His Word. "…You do not have because you do not ask God. (James 4:2)." Because of this misconception we feel that we either haven't done enough to deserve the promise (works…not grace) or aren't important enough to get His attention (favoritism).

I believe that there is one thing that separates us and the saints of the Bible. That is expectation. Abraham acted on the promise of God because he EXPECTED it to happen. Noah EXPECTED God to send rain. They all EXPECTED that what God said was true. And it is no different with us. The fulfillment of God's promises in our lives is dependent on us not on God. "But when you ask, you must believe and not doubt…(James 1:6)." If God did it for Abraham…He'll do it for me. If He did it for David…He'll do it for me. If He did it for Peter, Paul, John, the disciples, and apostles…He'll do it for me. All we need to do is expect them to happen.

DAY 14

One evening not long ago I had a particularly difficult time. Let's just say that my nerves were definitely frazzled by the time I went to bed. As I laid down to go to sleep there were two thoughts that went through my mind. The first was a prayer. "Oh, God, help me to give this to you so I can rest tonight." That's exactly what I prayed. The second thought was, "I hope I can sleep tonight."

I've said it before and I'll say it again…trouble comes when we least expect it. We can be relaxing and recharging in the green pasture that God has led us to and all of the sudden this weed sprouts up and the lush, green landscape is marred. Yet there is something that can occur when the weeds sprout that is simply amazing. "And the peace of God, which transcends all understanding, will guard your hearts and your minds in Christ Jesus. (Philippians 4:7)"

I'm not a really big fan of yard work. I understand that it is necessary but I still don't like it. My idea of a perfect yard is one that everyone admires and someone else maintains (but it's still my yard). But we all know that unless you hire a gardener to maintain the yard you have to do it yourself. But wait…what did Jesus say? "I am the true vine, and my Father is the gardener. (John 15:1)" While God may not totally deal with the weeds He has the knowledge to guide us through dealing with them.

Look at the verse in Philippians again. The word transcends means, "to rise above or go beyond; overpass; exceed." Just like the gardener that helps you deal with weeds in the yard the peace of God helps us deal with 'weeds' in life, even when we may not know or understand how to. Now…here's where it gets really cool. The word guard in that verse means, "to guard, protect by a military guard, either to prevent hostile invasion, or to keep the inhabitants of a besieged city from flight." It's a picture of the sentinel that walked the city walls and looked out on the horizon to warn the city of impending trouble. In essence this verse is saying that the peace of God will watch over your life. It will warn you when trouble comes so that the peace that you enjoy is not interrupted. To put it another way…it gives you the know how to deal with the weeds in the green pasture when you don't know how on your own.

This just what I needed that night. I needed God to walk in and help me deal with stuff so that I could sleep. I needed peace. And the cool thing is…the next thing I remember after praying, "God, help me sleep." was the alarm going off to wake me up. I'm still enjoying the green pastures. I just have to deal with some weeds here and there. I also know that if He does that for me…He will do it for anyone.

DAY 15

Not long ago I was listening to Dr. Tony Evans' podcast on angels. He is a national best-selling author, teacher, and pastor of Oak Cliff Bible Fellowship in Dallas, Texas. It's really worth a listen. He said something that has been rolling around in my mind and I can't get away from it. He said (and I'm paraphrasing), "When the devil wants to do something to you he has to get permission from God first." Now I'll be honest with you...that goes against everything that I've been taught my whole life. But as I began to look at it again I see that on some levels it is correct.

I believe that all too often we think that the devil has free reign in our life to test and try us as he wants to do. But after looking at scripture this mindset is incorrect. The Bible teaches us that we are ambassadors of Christ (2 Corinthians 5:20). It also teaches that we are adopted into God's family (Romans 8:15). These two things alone reveal something that we forget all too often. If someone knows Christ they don't belong to this world — and consequently the devil can't touch us without permission from God.

We see examples of this throughout Scripture. Two places that are evident are in Luke 22:31 and Job chapter 1. In both accounts the devil had to ask permission before doing anything to God's people.

He doesn't have free reign to test and try and afflict at his whim. We fall under the protection of Almighty God! So how then does the enemy touch us? I believe there are two primary ways that he gains access to us.

The first is what we like to call tests or trials. James talks about these tests in the first chapter. These are things that are brought about to test our faith. James says to "…consider it pure joy…" when these things come along. While they may not be pleasant things a test always means that you're ready to move on. To advance to the next rank (or belt) in martial arts there is a test to see whether you've learned all the necessary techniques. The tests in life are not any different. That's why we need to count it all joy when the trials come. God is testing us so that we can advance into deeper things in Him. And there are always limits applied to the tests. God always sets boundaries (1 Corinthians 10:13).

The second way that he gains access is through our choices. "and do not give the devil a foothold. (Ephesians 4:27)" The word 'foothold' here means opportunity, power, occasion for acting. Opportunity for what? Opportunity to test, try, and afflict. You see…when we make a choice to step out from under the umbrella of God's protection we are presenting the devil with an opportunity. And he is on the prowl for those (1 Peter 5:8). So the next time we see a trial in life there are only two places to look (as long as you know Christ). One of two people gave the devil permission to touch you. Either God did or you did. The devil doesn't have free reign to touch you. He has to have permission first.

DAY 16

I'm not a very good Facebooker (is that even a word). I get on every once in a while to post a status or look and see what people are doing. Most of the time, to be honest, it just annoys me. People just put anything on their page. It doesn't have to be relevant to anything happening. Oh, by the way, if I offend anyone that loves Facebook it wasn't intended. My point is that I recently posted this status, "I am always amazed at the excitement and nervousness that occurs when God takes us out of our comfort zone." I posted it because God is stirring something in me that takes me way past anything that I thought would ever be possible. And it's a stretch.

My choice of exercise is to practice martial arts, specifically Tae Kwon Do. I currently hold the rank of purple belt and am striving towards my first black belt. I have about a year or so until I can start thinking about testing for it. My goal is to have my second black belt and be working on my third by the time I'm 50. That gives me 10 years in case anyone is wondering. I mention this because one of the very important things in martial arts is stretching. If you don't stretch…you can't kick at the necessary levels to progress. And you run the risk of hurting yourself — very badly in some cases. Stretching is not my favorite part of the workouts. In some cases it hurts —

a lot. But if I continue to stretch then I know it can only help me in my endeavors to improve and progress. And it brings me that much closer to my goal.

Back to my Facebook status. When God moves us to new things it can be unnerving. There's some apprehension, sometimes some nervousness, maybe some excitement, and definitely some pain. None of these are fun. It's not what we're used to. And it definitely hurts. But it's necessary. Remember what James wrote, "Consider it pure joy, my brothers and sisters, whenever you face trials of many kinds, because you know that the testing of your faith produces perseverance. Let perseverance finish its work so that you may be mature and complete, not lacking anything. (James 1:2-4)"

Master Williams (my TKD instructor) asks me to assist in teaching the kid's class that immediately precedes the one I'm in. Without fail, when we're warming up and stretching, I hear one of the kids say, "But it hurts!" And they're right. It hurts to stretch. It hurts to move outside that which makes us comfortable. But when we do the results are amazing. It's not any different when God moves us. He is stretching our faith, abilities, trust, and a host of other things. And it hurts. Yet it strengthens all of these things and more. Our confidence in God and who we are in Him skyrockets when we come out on the other side. That's why James wrote what he did. When the trials and tests come…be happy. Look forward to the stretches and embrace them because they're only preparing you for bigger and better things.

DAY 17

In 2 Kings 5 we read the story of Naaman. He was the commander of the army of Aram. But there was something wrong. He had leprosy. And in those days there was no cure for this disease. Naaman was a marked man for life. Yet in all things we see the hand of God working.

"Now bands of raiders from Aram had gone out and had taken captive a young girl from Israel, and she served Naaman's wife. (2 Kings 5:2)" Here's where we see the beginning of God's working. How can I say that? Well…if this girl hadn't been serving Naaman's wife…she couldn't have told them about the prophet. It always amazes me how God works outside of what we expect or know (more on that in a bit). We tend to forget what God says about this…"'For my thoughts are not your thoughts, neither are your ways my ways,' declares the Lord. (Isaiah 55:8)"

So…after a confusing string of events…Naaman hooks up with the prophet and here's what he's told. "Elisha sent a messenger to say to him, 'Go, wash yourself seven times in the Jordan, and your flesh will be restored and you will be cleansed.' (2 Kings 5:10)" Woo Hoo!! All he has to do is wash up and he's good to go. It seems like

Naaman should be running for the river. But instead he gets mad. Really? He's handed the answer to a huge problem in his life and he gets mad because it's not what he expected. "...I thought that he would surely come out to me and stand and call on the name of the Lord his God, wave his hand over the spot and cure me of my leprosy. (2 Kings 5:11)"

There's only one difference between us and ancient Israel. Do you want to know what it is? Technology. They didn't have indoor plumbing, cell phones, tablets, or the internet. Other than that...we're all the same. We think like they did and act like they did. How do I know that? Because I've done the same thing that Naaman did. I've gotten mad because God didn't do something like I thought He should do it. And if you're honest with yourself...so have you.

But there's a danger in Naaman's reaction. He risks missing out on the miracle from God. What if Naaman hadn't listened to his servant and had went home to his rivers? What would have happened to the blind man if he refused to wash in the pool after Jesus put the mud on his eyes (John 9)? You see God will work in the way that brings Him the most glory. The credit belongs to Him. We have to be careful that we're not so set in how we want something done that we miss out on the actual miracle.

The Bible is packed with promises that God will take care of us, guide us, and watch over us. What it doesn't say is how He will do it. If we learn to trust Him in the middle of it the outcome will be nothing short of a miracle.

DAY 18

"Can any one of you by worrying add a single hour to your life? (Matthew 6:27)" Worry…it's something we tell ourselves not to do. Yet we do it all the time. And to some of us its hold is inescapable. It can steal our focus, destroy our hope, and sap our strength. It disturbs our life, our peace, and — in some cases — our confidence. It does us no good yet we still do it.

Worry is defined as, "to torment oneself with or suffer from disturbing thoughts." And this torment is usually self-inflicted. We let our mind run over and over the 'what ifs' and let them play out over and over in our mind. All to our detriment. According to WebMD excessive worrying can cause some pretty serious physical complications. Not only does it affect us physically but it can affect us emotionally and mentally as well.

So how do we stop this? Is there anything we can do? Can we really live a worry free life? I believe that we really can. It will take discipline, self-control, and the courage to face the issue head on. But if we do…we can conquer a very dangerous enemy. Here's some ways we can do it.

Turn it over to God. Let's face it…we all want to be independent. We all want to do things on our own. Life has a way of getting really big, really fast though. And sometimes we just need to give it up and ask for help. God wants to help us with the worries and cares of life (1 Peter 5:7) so why not turn them over to Him? If we do this sooner than later we will save ourselves a lot of stress and strain.

Don't pick up the worry again. I'm really good at doing this. I turn something over to God and then take it back from Him. It goes like this for a while until I exhaust myself. Then in desperation I throw it on God hoping that He'll take it back. Why do I do this? Honestly, I'm not quite sure. But I bet I'm not the only one that does it. We need to have the confidence in God that says, "I'm turning this over to you one time. It's yours. Please work it out and give me peace in the process." And when we do that He promises that He will work it out for our good.

Control what you think about. Philippians 4 verse 8 gives us a list of things to think about. Things that are true and noble, right and pure, lovely and admirable. Worry is not any of these things. It's your mind. Don't let it run you! Instead "…take captive every thought to make it obedient to Christ. (2 Corinthians 10:5)"

It's a continuing battle in all of us. But we can't change circumstances by worrying about them. It doesn't extend our life (it shortens it if we're not careful). This battle can, however, be won if we will put our mind to it. Really…what do we have to worry about anyway? I'm thinking that when God is there…not much.

DAY 19

"But seek first his kingdom and his righteousness, and all these things will be given to you as well. (Matthew 6:33)" I've heard this verse many times over the past few months. Normally God is trying to get me to see something so I try to sit up and take notice. As I began to think about this verse I started thinking about the "other things". We all like the other things. And that's perfectly ok. But if we're not careful we can switch the focus of this verse.

God does everything in order. He created the universe in a specific order. He set up his commandments in order. The Earth rotates around the sun, the moon around the Earth. All of it is set in motion in a specific order. When we look at this verse it has an order to it as well. It goes like this…God first, then the rest of life. Although it's simple we can really get ourselves in a jam if we don't follow it.

You see, I believe that we have a different idea of what the "other things" are. When we look at life and all its circumstances and situations we can form our own list of the other things that we need. Having more money to pay the bills would be great. A bigger house to live in would give us more room. A more reliable car to get me where

I need to go. None of these things in themselves are wrong to have…but what happens when we receive them? Does the receipt of these things nullify our reliance on God?

I'm learning that reliance on God for the other things is good…as long as we look for the right "other things". Seeking God first doesn't mean that the bill won't get paid. It just means that we seek Him to be our Provider. It means that we seek Him to be our Peace when the stress and worry of life rears its head. It means that we desire His grace and mercy in our life because we have put Him first. And the funny thing about seeking Him first is that if we truly make that our life's passion the things we want and desire change. We no longer have to ask God to move in the cares of life because He already has them in His hands –because we put them there. Our desires are fulfilled because our desires become His desires.

I'm reminded of an old song that my grandma used to sing in church. She absolutely loved this one. It goes…"Turn your eyes upon Jesus. Look full in His wonderful face. And the things of Earth will grow strangely dim, in the light of His glory and grace." That pretty much sums up the verse. Put Jesus first. Then this, that, and the "other things" will all be ok. Why? He promised they would. And Jesus knows how to keep His promises.

DAY 20

Dreams are interesting things. No, I'm not talking about the ones caused by too much pizza before bed. Let's face it...those ones can get downright weird. The dreams that I am thinking of aren't really ones that you have at night while sleeping. I'm talking about those things that you want to accomplish. Some would call them goals or ambitions. They're the things that you think about. The things that you say, "I really want to do this." These dreams can be powerful. For some...they can be a life changing thing.

We think about goals, dreams, and desires all the time. Some would like more money. Some would like a different job. Some would like to meet Mr. or Miss Right. But have we really thought about life and the things it entails...about the people we touch and impact? When we really look at it we don't have all that much time here on Earth and, I believe, that we can spend too much time chasing after dreams that don't really matter. After all...according to Scripture, "Why, you do not even know what will happen tomorrow.

What is your life? You are a mist that appears for a little while and then vanishes. (James 4:14)"

As I began thinking about dreams my mind started to focus on all the people in the Bible that had a dream.

- Abraham had a dream and he became the father of Israel.
- Joseph had a dream and he saved an entire nation.
- Jacob had a dream and it changed his identity.

The Bible is full of people who had dreams (remember...we're talking about goals and ambitions here) that, when attained, changed not only their life but the lives of those around them. When you really look at the origin of those dreams we see why they had such an impact. They were God-given dreams.

When we look at the dreams that we want to accomplish are we looking at the things that God has for us? Or are we letting life get in the way and dictate what our dreams are? I believe that too many of us allow our dreams to be dictated by our circumstances. And when we do that we miss out on huge, life changing things that would make us stop and say, "Wow!" See we forget what God says about dreams. "'For I know the plans I have for you,' declares the Lord, 'plans to prosper you and not to harm you, plans to give you hope and a future.' (Jeremiah 29:11)"

God has dreams for us too. And His dreams go way beyond more money or a better house. They go far past a better job. They totally bypass the new car. They're dreams to bring about the best in you so people can see Him. They're dreams like the ones He gave Abraham. The one that said, "I'm going to make something great out of you." God's dreams don't take the easy road. In fact he sometimes walks us through some pretty tough times (look at the individuals mentioned above). But if we embrace His dreams for us…the impact will be something that we never imagined or expected. They just may make us sit back and say…WOW!

DAY 21

One of the marks of a great relationship is that you miss the other person when you spend an extended amount of time apart. You find yourself thinking more and more about the next time you will see them. It almost occupies all of your time. I've known some people who almost make it an obsession.

As I was rolling this thought around in my head I began to ask myself if I miss God when we don't spend time together. I know this may come as a shock…so brace yourself…but I don't always spend the time with God that I should or want to. If we're honest with ourselves we'd all have to say the same thing. Not even David (the writer of many of the Psalms…man after God's heart) spent the kind of time he really wanted to. It's evident when we read verses like, "My soul thirsts for God, for the living God. When can I go and meet with God?" (Psalm 42:2)

I remember one especially busy week that I had. It was one of those blink and it's gone kind of weeks. You know what I'm talking about, I'm sure. Not only were the days booked…but the nights were too. The next week we started special services for our church in California. When I walked into that service and the music started I remember God whispering to me, "I've missed you." Right then it felt like God walked up to me and wrapped me in a big hug. If you've never had a hug from God…it's something to experience. I'll never forget it. I'll also never forget how I felt when I realized that God missing me was my fault.

I began to realize that even the shortest moments with God can be so wonderfully intimate. We don't have to spend 4 hours on our knees every day. We just need to realize that God wants to be involved with us. He delights in the details of our lives (Psalm 37:23 — NLT). Since that's true (it must be since it's written in the Bible) shouldn't we want to include God in everything? Shouldn't we miss Him when we spend time away from Him? Here's the cool thing, though. Since God is always present we don't have to spend extended time away from Him. We have the ability to talk with and hear from Him throughout the days, weeks, and years of our lives. When we set our mind to spending that time with God He immediately takes notice and rushes to keep the appointment…because He adores that time with us.

DAY 22

I've seen friends and acquaintances posting things they are thankful for on Facebook — one a day for the month of November. I think it's sort of a cool thing. It makes us focus on the great things that are going on in our life rather than the not so good things. I have learned one thing over the past couple of years though. Don't discount the bad things in our lives...they are more valuable than we realize.

There's a scene at the end of one episode of Star Trek: The Next Generation (yeah, I'm a bit of a Trekkie) that really shows us how true this is. Jean Luc Picard (played by Patrick Stewart) got the opportunity to change some of the things in his life and it dramatically altered how it turned out. He said the following about those things: "I always looked at my life as having loose threads, unruly things that I thought needed to be cleaned up. But when I pulled on one of those threads it unwove the tapestry that is my life." Wow! What a statement.

Getting back to the thirty days of being thankful...I think it's very important to look at all the great things in our life. It shows us how truly blessed we are. I don't think, however, that we should totally ignore the struggles either. God uses many of these struggles to bring about some of our greatest blessings.

Over the past two years I have experienced some of the darkest times in my entire life. Honestly there were times that I didn't think I would survive. But here I am…on the other side. And God taught me so much about who He is and about myself. I know he could have taught me without having gone through these things; and I don't think He caused them; but He used the bad things to bring me closer to Him. One major thing I've learned is to ask **what** He's doing instead of **why** it's happening. I believe that this is a lesson that we all could learn. We have heard the songs like *Blessing In the Thorn* by Phillips, Craig, & Dean, *Jesus Bring The Rain* by Mercy Me, and *Blessings* by Laura Story. They dwell on the 'what' rather than the 'why'. It's never said that the struggles are easy but that God reveals Himself through them.

One thing God revealed to me in the midst of these struggles is that He reveals to us who He is in the midst of these things. When we're in trouble…He's our Deliverer. When we're hurting…He's our Healer. When we're worried or afraid…He's our peace. And every time we go through something else it's an opportunity for God to reveal Himself in a deeper way.

I have a lot to be thankful for. I have wonderful kids and a great job. I'm healthy. I'm happy. Life is pretty good. But if you ask me what I'm most thankful for my gut-level honest answer really would have to be: "All of it…the good and bad."

DAY 23

I grew up in church and have heard 'church phrases' my entire life. It seems like we have a phrase for everything. Feeling down? "The joy of the Lord is your strength." Worried about something? "Don't worry about anything, just pray about it." Facing a difficult decision? "Just trust God for the answer." It's that last one that really has me thinking lately.

We all know what trust is. Just in case, though, here's the definition: reliance on the integrity, strength, ability, surety, etc., of a person or thing; confidence. It's not normally something that we just throw around. We don't trust just anyone. We don't trust the person we just met at the grocery store. We don't really trust the friend of a friend we met at a party (not with everything). Trust is built over time…as a relationship grows.

So how is it, then, that we say trust God with some of the biggest things in our lives when we, in most cases, don't really know Him? If trust is built over a period of getting to know someone…shouldn't we get to know God so we can trust Him? I assure you that this is one of His deepest desires…to know you and for you to know Him.

I'm also reminded of another verse that ties into this. Jesus said that unless we become like a child we cannot enter the Kingdom of Heaven. Again…I started thinking about this and how it relates to the trust thing. Here's what I figured out. I always pictured this verse talking about being innocent like a child. And in some ways that's true. But have we ever seen children interacting with their father? There's a trust there that is like no other. I, myself, have played with my children in ways that required their complete trust in me. Things like…

- Jumping into the pool and assuring them that I won't let them get hurt.
- Running alongside of them while they're learning to ride their bike so I'll catch them if they fall.
- Picking them up when they want me to hold them and trusting that I can handle their weight and won't drop them.

Not once did their trust ever waiver. Not once did they question whether I would be there. Not once did they falter or fail in their confidence in their dad. And that trust was not misplaced. I believe that this is one of the things that we need to be childlike about with God. We jump because we know that He will catch us. We run knowing that he is running right beside us. We crawl in His lap knowing that He's there to hold us when we need it.

This is the trust that I believe God really wants us to have in Him. It's not an easy thing to do. In fact it's one of the hardest things for us to do. But I guarantee that if we become childlike in that trust …it won't be misplaced. After all he is God.

DAY 24

Afriend of mine posted a verse on Facebook that really caught my attention. It is a verse in the Psalms...specifically Psalm 18:16. "He reached down from heaven and rescued me; he drew me out of deep waters. (NLT)" As I read this verse the first phrase jumped off the screen and almost slapped me in the face. Not a bad slap...but a get-your-attention kind of thing.

We reach for things every day. Many times we don't give it a second thought. We reach for our keys. We reach for our wallet or purse. We reach for the power button on the computer. Every day, multiple times a day, our hand reaches for something. There are times, though, that our reach is intentional. We reach for our children or grandchildren to tell them we love them. We reach for our spouse to show some affection. We reach for a friend's hand to shake it.

Sometimes our reaching isn't to anyone on this planet. There are times that we reach out to God for something. Maybe it's because of something that is needed — comfort, provision, or protection. Maybe it's to show love or affection toward Him. Maybe it's to introduce yourself and ask that He be a part of your life. But whatever the reason...we're reaching out.

Nothing has taught me more about God than being a father. I have learned about loving regardless of behavior. I have learned the difficulty in disciplining. I have learned that when they hurt I hurt. There have been times that I've had to quickly reach out to my kids and 'pull them out' of something because it would bring great harm to them. All of these things reflect how God is toward us.

We see examples of God reaching out throughout the Bible. He reached out to thwart the enemies of Israel. He reached out to provide an heir for Abraham. In each situation, when God reached out, it was on purpose. Jesus did the same thing. He reached out to calm the raging sea. He reached out to heal diseases and raise the dead. He reached out to pull Peter from the stormy waters. He reached out His hand to put it on a cross. All of these were done on purpose, for a purpose.

There are times when He reaches out to us as well. We see this most clearly in the Psalms.

- He lifted me out of the slimy pit, out of the mud and mire...(Psalm 40:2)
- ...he drew me out of deep waters. (Psalm 18:16)

When God reaches nothing can stop it. Death can't stop it. Illness can't stop it. Depression and poverty can't stop it. All it takes is God reaching and things move and happen. Where do we need God to reach out for us? What do we need Him to touch? How do we need Him to respond? All it takes is reaching out; on purpose with one goal…reaching God. He promises that He will hear and answer. Because God loves it when we reach for Him. And He always reaches back.

DAY 25

I'm going to ask a question that I already know the answer to. But I'm going to ask it anyway. Has anyone ever messed up? I mean really, really bad? I thought so. We all have. So…how did that make you feel? Yeah, I know the answer to that one too. Not all that good, huh? It didn't make me feel too great either.

Recently I made a mistake. That mistake had the potential to do some pretty big damage. Fortunately the people involved are loving, kind, and forgiving. But it still weighed on my mind and heart. How could I have done that? Why did I ignore the situation? Why didn't I just take care of it earlier? Do any of these questions sound familiar? I would wager that they do. And they all have one thing in common. Guilt. We feel guilty for the mistakes that we make.

Guilt is an interesting thing. It easily locks us up in the prison of 'If only.' If only I had made a different decision. If only I hadn't done that one thing. It's a lonely place…the prison of 'If only.' And guilt never comes alone. It always brings a friend. "Let me introduce you to someone," says guilt. "This is regret." "Don't you feel bad," hisses regret. "You should have known better. But you can't go back and change it." And they go on and on making us feel worse and worse about the mistake we made. We retreat deeper and deeper into the prison; willingly walking through the halls into solitary confinement. And we shut the door ourselves.

But is there a way to avoid being imprisoned? There sure is! While it's a hard thing to battle we must understand that guilt and regret can only work on us if we let them. We step into the cell. We stay in prison. I'm not saying that we need to ignore issues that need to be dealt with. But once they are...move on. It's done and no good can come from beating ourselves up over past mistakes.

A reason that guilt and regret are so devastating in us is that they keep us from moving forward. They anchor us to past mistakes by making us relive them over and over. This causes us to stop being effective in life because our focus is now on something that we can't change.

- Forget the former things; do not dwell on the past. (Isaiah 43:18)
- Therefore, if anyone is in Christ, the new creation has come: The old has gone, the new is here! (2 Corinthians 5:17)

If it's done, understand that it's done. We can't change the mistake...we can only learn from it and move on. Life will be full of mistakes and missteps. But we don't have to condemn ourselves for past mistakes. God doesn't. "Therefore, there is now no condemnation for those who are in Christ Jesus, (Romans 8:1)" The difference between condemnation and conviction is pretty easy to see. Condemnation pushes or pulls us away from the cross. On the other hand, conviction draws people towards the cross.

So…if you're an inmate imprisoned by guilt and regret for a past mistake, I challenge you to walk out of that cell. They can't hold you there. Staying in jail only hurts you. It's time to set yourself free. Your sentence has been overturned.

DAY 26

"But the swamps and marshes will not become fresh; they will be left for salt. (Ezekiel 47:11)" The start of Ezekiel chapter 47 tells of a river of fresh water that flows from the throne of God. Everywhere this river flows we see life and growth. The water nourishes the vegetation and encourages life. It even turns a portion of the Dead Sea into a place that can sustain living creatures in the water. That's a pretty powerful thing! Out of this passage there are two things that God has been telling me and I believe that they may help someone else.

Number one...*God can turn anything around.* As I thought about these verses (and reread them) something caught my attention. If you know anything about the Dead Sea in Israel you understand that it is incapable of sustaining life. The salt content of the water is so high that nothing can live in it. Hence the name — Dead Sea. Some things in our lives mirror the Dead Sea. It's so painful, stressful, discouraging, oppressing, and so on that no good can come out of it. Yet we see that even the Dead Sea is capable of springing to life when God intervenes.

Job — we all know who he is — faced devastating losses. Yet the end of his life was more blessed than the beginning. Elijah faced a death threat and ran for his life…but when he returned he mentored Elisha. Elisha, by the way, performed twice as many miracles as Elijah did. We see example after example of God turning circumstances around and using them for His glory. "I am the Lord, the God of all mankind. Is anything too hard for me? (Jeremiah 32:27)" I'm thinking no on that one.

Number two…*if we dwell on our struggles they will keep us from experiencing the freshness of God's move.* Dwelling on past hurts and pain only leads to more hurt and pain. When we do that it shifts our focus from a loving God that wants to teach us how great He really is. The focus stays on the hurt and pain and it lingers until we are caught in the middle of a swampy mess of bitterness and discouragement. And let's be honest the next thing coming is a pity party and no one ever RSVP's to those.

While hurt, pain, and discouragement are not fun we need to embrace the things that they can teach us about ourselves. If a child touches a hot stove they learn that it will burn them and they won't touch it again. It's not a good thing that they got hurt but they learned a valuable lesson from it. We need to let God teach us the lessons from our hurt, pain, and discouragement and turn those things into fresh lessons that He can use for His glory. No one wants to live in a swamp. Get out! Leave it behind and start living in the fresh things that God has for you.

If I'm given a choice between eating a stale, crusty doughnut that

I have at my house or a fresh, soft, warm one at the shop…I'll choose the latter every time. Do the same thing in life. Don't get caught in the swamp. Understand that God can do **anything**. Start experiencing new life from the Dead Sea circumstances.

DAY 27

I've been thinking a lot about prayer. Mostly about how I pray. The conclusion that I have come up with is that it really needs to change. I'm not saying that I'm praying for anything out of the ordinary. Quite the contrary in fact. The things I'm praying for are totally normal. I bring the emotional, mental, spiritual, and financial needs to God all the time. That's what I'm supposed to do…right? But lately I find that something is missing.

What God is starting to show me is that bringing my needs to Him is good. His Word tells me to do just that. In fact we quote the verses all the time. "Do not be anxious about anything, but in every situation, by prayer and petition, with thanksgiving, present your requests to God (Philippians 4:6)" We love to bring our stuff to God because He tells us to. We "…cast all our cares on Him…" and He wants us to do that. But is there more? Can prayer be more than listing the things we need to God? Shouldn't we strive to know Him through the prayers we pray?

When I was a kid my Sunday School teacher (usually my grandmother — affectionately known as "Ma Maw") said that prayer is talking with God. It's a conversation and conversations shouldn't be one-sided. When we pray we need to allow time to hear what He is saying to us in the conversation. No other conversation that we have is this way. So why should it be any different with God?

I am reminded of Elijah when he ran from Jezebel in 1 Kings 19. At one point there is a gale force wind, boulder shattering earthquake, and blazing wildfire. But the Bible says that God was not in any of them. It then says, "…And after the fire came a gentle whisper. (1 Kings 19:12)" When Elijah heard it he covered his face with his cloak because he knew he was in the presence of God. That's the thing that we need to hear. We like to see the huge things that God does. But we also need to hear the whisper. A whisper is meant for only the person close enough to hear. And I think that's what's missing in many prayers around the world. We shout our prayers to God and fail to get close enough to hear the whisper.

So I challenge you to make your prayers into conversations. Present your requests to God. But also take the time to hear the whispers of God as he speaks to your heart. I promise that if you do…it will change your prayer time, and your life, forever.

DAY 28

A line from *The Karate Kid* with Jackie Chan got me thinking (something always does these days). He looked at his student and said, "Being still and doing nothing are two very different things." That's sermon material, baby! So I started thinking about the times that we see the phrase be still or stand still in the Bible.

There's the time at the Red Sea when Pharaoh's army was chasing the Israelites. There's the one where the army of Israel was severely outnumbered yet they went to battle anyway. There's the story of Jesus standing in the bow of the boat and telling the wind and waves to be still. All of these stories have one thing in common. Want to know what it is? Sure you do. But just in case...here you go.

In all these instances life was raging against people. The Israelites were being pursued to be put back into slavery. The Israelite army was fighting a war. A storm was raging that threatened to capsize the boat the disciples were in. At no point were the individuals doing nothing. In fact, quite the contrary was true. They all tried everything that they could to solve the issue at hand. All resources had been exhausted and they were out of options.

Any parent can relate to the phrase 'Be still'. It's something we tell our kids. What we really want from them, though, is to be quiet. This is the same thing we do with God. We get quiet and mistake it for stillness. In actuality all we're doing is being quiet. We're quietly worrying and fretting about the situation we're facing.

The word 'still' is defined as "free from turbulence or commotion; peaceful; tranquil; calm." If you read the entirety of the stories mentioned above these people were all but still. There was worrying, fretting, anxiousness, and a whole lot of other things going on. Nothing else could be done and they were in trouble. Yet we see God Almighty telling them to 'Be Still'. Really?!? You want me to do nothing?

I believe it could be reworded 'Be at peace'. When God stepped in…the situation immediately changed. The impassable sea could be walked through. The mighty enemy was miraculously defeated. The raging storm was calmed. Though they were out of options…God never was. So when He brought the miracle (and each of these deliverances was a miracle) the people could see that no matter what happens God could always be counted on.

Fast forward to our lives. What things are raging in us? What options have been exhausted? Have we come to a dead end? Well, God says the same thing to you and me…"Be still." It's not doing nothing. Far from it. It's really letting God do His thing while life rages against us. When we let Him do that He walks us right through the situation and we're at peace the whole time.

DAY 29

We tend to define peace in pictures. We say things like, "I slept peacefully last night." Or we might look at it like being in a grassy meadow with the sunshine warming our face while we relax. Not bad huh? I could definitely go for some of that. But isn't that view a little skewed? It's a little too perfect; a little too unattainable. After all…which one of us ever has time to sit in a grassy meadow for any length of time?

Most of us find ourselves in the predicament that Peter was in. He rushes in without thinking and then, when life rages against him, he falters. We all know the story (but I'll summarize it anyway). Jesus tells the disciples to go to the other side of the lake while he goes to pray. In the middle of the night, in a huge storm, we see Jesus walking out to the boat on the water. The disciples are all freaked out. Well, all except Peter. He wants to do what Jesus is doing. So Jesus invites him out.

That's where things take a turn. Peter is walking along, doing the impossible. He steps out on the water and doesn't sink. All is well.

Cool! But then he sees the situation he's in. In reality, what happens is his head gets in the way. He sees the wind and huge waves and sinks.

That's where many of us find ourselves. We're walking along just fine and then life starts raging against us. Which sorta brings me to the point of all of this. Many people just try to deal with it as best as they can. The goal is to get through it, to survive. But I believe that we can do more than survive. I believe that God wants to work right in the middle of our storm.

Jesus said in John 14: 27, "Peace I leave with you; my peace I give you. I do not give to you as the world gives. Do not let your hearts be troubled and do not be afraid." So this begs the question...how is Jesus' peace different? Well, Jesus was in the same storm that Peter was. He was walking on the same lake. He saw the same waves and felt the same wind. Yet Jesus was able to walk on the water without sinking. I know, I know...Jesus was God. But he said that he gives us His peace. So it must be different.

So different it is, in fact, that it allows us to do the same things that He did. We can walk through the howling, raging, fierceness of life's challenges. And instead of sinking like Peter did...we can walk on top of it just like Jesus did. All because we choose His peace. It's a peace that goes beyond our understanding. It calms the most frazzled nerves. It relieves the deepest worry. It soothes the darkest fear. How? Because it's from God. That's the kind of peace I want. How about you?

DAY 30

"**A**nd now, dear brothers and sisters, one final thing. Fix your thoughts on what is true, and honorable, and right, and pure, and lovely, and admirable. Think about things that are excellent and worthy of praise. (Philippians 4:8 – NLT)" Fix your thoughts...what a cool statement. Another word that can be used is meditate. Now when we hear that word, many times, it conjures up pictures of monks or priests sitting on the floor with their arms crossed moaning "Ohm". In reality, though, that's not what meditation is.

Meditate is defined as: to engage in thought or contemplation; reflect. Simply put — fixing our minds on something. If we're honest with ourselves we do this all the time. It's called worrying. We worry (meditate) about our job. We worry (meditate) about our kids and their school work. We worry (meditate) about the car repairs or the bills. We're always meditating (worrying) on something.

David had this meditation thing down pat. He constantly wrote about it...

- Within your temple, O God, we **meditate** on your unfailing love. (Psalm 48:9)

- I will consider all your works and **meditate** on all your mighty deeds. (Psalm 77:12)

- I **meditate** on your precepts and consider your ways. (Psalm 119:15)

Meditation is not a bad thing. It's not something from eastern religion that will draw us away from God. It can bring us closer to Him. And we are actually encouraged to do it constantly. Joshua admonishes us to "...**meditate** on it [God's Word] day and night. (Joshua 1:8)" Paul encourages us to think about good things. All throughout the Bible we see examples of meditation being given.

You see, the thing about this is that we become what we think about. Remember the old saying "Garbage in, garbage out"? It really is true. What we really think about/meditate on comes out in all we do. Stressful, worried thinking leads us to stressful, worried lives. And that's not what God wants for us! He wants us to live a life full of peace and joy and it all starts with what is running through our brain. "You will keep in perfect peace those whose minds are steadfast, because they trust in you. (Isaiah 26:3)" Hmmm...doesn't that sound like something you want? Perfect peace. Wow! It can be yours...just think about the right things.

I know what you're thinking right now. You're saying, "I can't just think about certain things." I would disagree with that. What we think about is totally up to us. This is exactly why Paul tells us what to think about in Philippians. The things we think about are our choice. We choose whether we're going to worry or trust God. Choose the things to think about and "fix your thoughts" on God. That's the path that leads to a life full of peace, joy, and all the other good stuff.

DAY 31

Gifts. We all like to get them. There's nothing wrong with that. It's basic human nature to like getting something from someone else. I especially enjoy watching my children receive gifts — whether on their birthday, Christmas, or any other occasion. The question is, though, whether we like giving as much as getting.

Getting stuff is a big part of our culture. It's so big, in fact, that most of America is in debt up to their eyeballs to get that stuff. But what do we do about the stuff we can't get in a store? It's not stocked on any shelves or listed in a catalog or on Amazon. You can't put it on lay away. It can't be wrapped up in pretty paper. Well…you get the idea. While many of us appear to be living the high life…we're actually living in poverty because we're missing the things that we really need.

I was listening to Dave Ramsey and he was talking about living generously. While the focus was mainly on money (because that's what he deals with)…I believe that we can live generously in other ways as well. Jesus even taught this. He said, "Give, and it will be given to you. A good measure, pressed down, shaken together and running over, will be poured into your lap. For with the measure you use, it will be measured to you. (Luke 6:38)" What is it? Well…it is what you need. If something is missing maybe you need to give that very thing so that it can come back to you. If you need some kindness…try giving a little first. If you need some encouragement…try giving some first. If you need some guidance…try giving some first.

When I was a teenager one of my summer and after school jobs was working at a 7-11 store. One of my favorite things in the store was the banana Slurpee. Wow…are they good! If you've never had one…there's something you need to know about them. When you pour them into the cup they expand. If you're not careful what looks like enough will quickly overflow and get all over the place. It's no different with generosity. When we begin to apply this principle there is a promise. What we give will come back in measures that are more than we need. Paul wrote to the Ephesians that God "… is able to do immeasurably more than all we ask or imagine…(Ephesians 3:20)"

We can't, however, ignore the last part of the verse in Luke. "…For with the measure you use, it will be measured to you." Remember that we're talking about being generous. We can't expect God to use a snow shovel to pour out His blessings when we give with a teaspoon. Don't be afraid to be generous with the kindness, guidance, encouragement, or whatever else is that you need. When God sees that he begins to heap those very things back on us in immeasurable quantities. And then we can give away the excess and the process starts all over again!

So…what is it that you need? Maybe it's missing because God is waiting on you to give it out first. Go ahead…try it. You might find "…It is more blessed to give than to receive. (Acts 20:35)"

DAY 32

I'm tired this morning. It was a busy weekend trying to move and doing yard work. When the alarm woke me up I silently wished for a hammer to turn it off. I shouldn't be tired but I am. I'm sure that almost everyone can relate to this feeling. A busy weekend or hectic day at work. A school program or ball practice. We all tend to run in more directions than we can count and it is exhausting. Usually we can recover if we just take a few moments to breathe or get to bed early one night and crash. Then it's back up again to continue the journey that we call life.

But what about the things that don't let us rest? Is there something we can do to battle the weariness that gets down deep and continually beats us up? You know what I'm talking about. It's the struggle with the teenage kid. Maybe it's the budget…or lack of. It could be marital struggles or job issues. Whatever it is…it lingers. And the weight is almost too much to bear.

"Even youths grow tired and weary, and young men stumble and fall; but those who hope in the Lord will renew their strength. They will soar on wings like eagles; they will run and not grow weary, they will walk and not be faint. (Isaiah 40:30-31)"

But those who hope in the Lord…what a statement. Even though we're tired and weary we can hope in the Lord. Nothing causes Him to get tired. Nothing rattles His confidence. Nothing confuses or frustrates Him. NOTHING! So what better place to put our hope?

The greatest thing about putting our hope in the Lord is that it goes way beyond circumstances. Even when we're tired and weary we can renew our strength…because it comes from the Lord. Right in the middle of the storm we can soar above it to get another perspective. We can continue to walk through the middle of the stuff and it won't wear us out. All because we put our hope in the Lord. Everyone else around us can be ready to throw in the towel, to give up because there's no hope, but we can continue on because our hope is in the Lord. "David was greatly distressed because the men were talking of stoning him; each one was bitter in spirit because of his sons and daughters. But David found strength in the Lord his God. (1 Samuel 30:6)"

I'm reminded of the story in Mark 9 where Jesus and the disciples crossed the sea. Jesus went to sleep in the back of the boat and the disciples took care of getting to the other side. But a storm caught them off guard and trouble started. The disciples finally woke Jesus up and he calmed the storm. That's what life is like for us sometimes. We're going along and all of a sudden something unexpected hits us; but Jesus is still in the boat with us. Nothing catches Him by surprise. Just when the disciples thought it was over…Jesus stepped in. They were safe because He was there.

DAY 33

We all like to get another shot at something. Whether that be to hit in the big game, dribble down the court, or sink the hole in one. No one likes to feel like a failure. Especially in life. But sometimes life can throw you a curve ball. You're laid off, finances take a turn and your home is foreclosed on, your marriage crumbles. Any number of things can happen that take you out of life. But God is always there.

If there's one thing I have learned it's that no one is immune to life and its tragedies. "…He causes his sun to rise on the evil and the good, and sends rain on the righteous and the unrighteous. (Matthew 5:45)" Everyone gets wet when it rains. Everyone sweats when it's hot. Knowing God doesn't give you a free pass out of trouble even though we may like it to sometimes.

I'm just one of those that would have liked to have a pass out of trouble. You see…the things I mentioned above have all touched my life (and then some). There was a time that I just thought it would be better if I didn't minister. The hurt was too great. The shame was too hard to bear. But God is always there. He walked me through the darkest time of my life and taught me something about Him and myself in the process. You've been reading about some of the things He taught me in other parts of this book. Yep...you guessed it...I'm a statistic. The day that my wife told me that she was done is burned into my brain — probably for the rest of my life. She was through. She wanted a divorce. And life changed.

But God is always there. In the midst of the biggest trial in my life...God revealed His grace and mercy to me in ways that I couldn't imagine. He taught me about myself and worshiping Him in the middle of it all. And just when I thought it couldn't get any better...he blessed me with something else. Or should I say someone else? July 6, 2013, will be my new wedding day. God brought a partner into my life that wants to walk the rest of it with me. I get another chance. Well, a new one.

In spite of all the stuff that life brings God still shines through. Nothing catches Him off guard or throws Him off of His game. He always knows just what's going on. While we may be confused about the future He is watching it unfold with confidence and clarity. Because God is always there. He is working on His plan. Teaching us, molding us, developing us. Smoothing out the rough edges that life can cause into a vessel that is worthy of the One that created it to begin with. So don't count yourself out just because life throws you a curve. Swing for the fence...because God is always there.

DAY 34

I'm going to ask a loaded question (because I already know the answer). Are you ready? "Have you ever felt like you're the only one dealing with a problem or situation?" Of course you have. We all have at one point or another. And you know what? It's normal. As long as there is trouble in this world we will all feel isolated. Even the prophet Elijah felt this way, "…I am the only one left, and now they are trying to kill me too. (1 Kings 19:10)" It's one of the tactics of the enemy to isolate us. Why? Because he knows that there's strength in numbers.

Our tendency, when we feel isolated, is to withdraw and wallow in our sorrow and misery. And you know what? That's exactly what the devil wants us to do! Why? Because when we do that we fail to use the tools that God gave us to combat this tactic. "What are these tools you speak of?" Well…I'm glad you asked.

1. Realize you're never alone. God's Word is packed with promises about us not ever being left alone. Trust that these promises are true because God's character won't allow Him to lie (see Numbers 23:19).

He refuses to leave us in the middle of situations by ourselves. When we're walking through something He is right there in the middle of it walking with us.

2. Throw it at God. "Cast all your anxiety on him because he cares for you. (1 Peter 5:7)" The word cast in the original Greek means to throw or place upon. This verse is telling us to throw our anxiety, issues, and problems at Him. It all comes down to trusting that God can handle the situation. And since He's the creator of the universe…I think He can.

3. Find a trusted person (in the family of God) to help you carry the load. This is probably the least used tool that God gave us. We're all, at some point or another, going to have problems, issues, trouble, stresses, worries, and more. Why in the world do we think we have to face them alone? We should all be willing to support each other in these tough times. And let's face it…we will all need to be supported too.

- "Rejoice with those who rejoice; mourn with those who mourn. (Romans 12:15)"
- "Carry each other's burdens, and in this way you will fulfill the law of Christ. (Galatians 6:2)"

There are more verses like this but suffice it to say that we're all part of God's family and family should stick together. God has given us so many things to fight the isolated, depressed, and lonely feelings that we inevitably face in life. The ones above are just a few. The important thing to remember is don't face it alone.

DAY 35

"Take delight in the Lord, and he will give you the desires of your heart. (Psalm 37:4)" I've heard this verse so much growing up. Many times I heard it quoted in reference to something that person really wanted. Now I'm not against wanting something. In fact...I'm all for it. We all want something. This is not a bad thing. Have we stopped and thought that there are things that God wants too?

The word desire is defined as: "a longing or craving, as for something that brings satisfaction or enjoyment." Something that satisfies. Hmmm...that really makes one think. What is it that satisfies? We all have such different definitions of something that satisfies. To one it may be money in the bank. To another...health. To another one possessions. The list is endless. But the question that we have to ask ourselves is whether these things can really satisfy. They can make us comfortable...that's for sure. Being comfortable and satisfied are two very different things though.

I remember praying about this very thing one day. I was bringing my list to God like I always did. After all…didn't He tell us to bring our requests before Him? But it's the thing that He spoke to me that really caught me off guard. He told me, "I'm tired of being a vending machine." A vending machine has no relationship with the customer. It is there to service the wants (not needs) of that person. In goes the money…and out comes the product. The person then walks away expecting that the machine will be there to service them again when they want something else. Wow! What a picture. God wants us to pray — even for our wants. But what He wants more than anything is us. His desire is the relationship. His desire is to know us and for us to know Him. And it's out of that relationship that our prayers should flow.

So…back to the beginning verse. I am convinced that when we pursue God rather than the stuff that satisfies our desires will change. They will morph into things that mirror what God wants. In other words, His desires become our desires. And then, when we begin to pray those desires, God is quick to answer and grant them. All because we pursued the relationship and allowed Him to change our heart. At that point the stuff that satisfies changes. It's like the old hymn says:

'Tis so sweet to trust in Jesus

Just to take Him at His word

Just to rest upon His Promise

And to know, "Thus saith the Lord."

DAY 36

One of my favorite verses is Psalm 37:23. In the New Living Translation it reads, "The Lord directs the steps of the Godly; He delights in every detail of their lives." We often think about God being involved in the really big things in life. Things like...where we should attend college or who we should marry. Or how about...finding the right place to live or what He has called us to do? All of us would agree that these things are all big decisions that need God's guidance.

Details – read smaller things here – are also important. It's the details that make a good picture great. Having the right combination of light and shadow will bring out the best parts of the photograph. Paying attention to the details when building a model gives those that view it the sense that it really is like the original. Job openings cite the importance of details when they post 'must be detail oriented'. One detail left unchecked in a contract can cause it to blow a multi-million dollar deal. The details in our lives are not any different. They affect every part of us – from what we wear to what we eat to how much sleep we get. Attention to detail in life is vastly important. One detail left unanswered can cause things to get out of control in a hurry.

We've heard the phrase, "The devil is in the details." I would have to disagree with that, however. According to the verse above…it's God who is in the details in our lives. The verse says he delights in them. In other words…he derives great pleasure from working out every area of our life. From keeping his hand on your dying late model car until that raise comes through…to where you will get the last $10 that you need to complete your missions trip fund…to whether you should make the purchase you've been contemplating.

I believe that God wants to be involved in the details because it's in the details that we can get to know Him and He can reveal Himself to us. The big things in life don't come around all that often. If we only involve God in the big things then we're missing out on so much more. If we push God out of the details we risk missing out on the beauty and pleasure of the sunrise. We fail to hear Him whispering in our ear that it's going to be ok and lose the joy that it brings.

Jesus said in John, "I have come that you might have life…" What's life if not a continuing set of changing details that need God's attention. The seasons need attention and the big things need attention but so do the details. So go ahead…I dare you…let God work on the details.

DAY 37

You're never alone. We've all heard that at one time or another. But if we're honest with ourselves we would admit that we have all, at one time or another, felt totally and completely alone. It's inevitable. We're faced with something that makes us feel isolated...like we're the only one dealing with these circumstances.

The feeling of being alone is a scary and depressing thing. It can sap the hope and joy from even the strongest individuals. And if the point of this was to make us all sad and hopeless...I would stop right here. But it's not. You see we're never alone. We always have someone in our corner working on our behalf. The Bible says in Romans 8:34 "...Christ Jesus who died—more than that, who was raised to life—is at the right hand of God and is also interceding for us."

The word intercede is an interesting one. In the English language it means, "to act or interpose in behalf of someone in difficulty or trouble, as by pleading or petition." In behalf of someone. That means Jesus is on your side. How cool is that?!? Jesus is talking to the

Father about all of the issues that you face right now. He is discussing with the Father all of the hurts that you face. He is bringing to the Father all of the worries that you face.

But wait…there's more! Not only is Jesus interceding on our behalf; He sent someone to stand in for us. "And I will ask the Father, and he will give you another advocate to help you and be with you forever— (John 14:6)." Do we really understand the meaning of this? We don't have one person in our corner…we have TWO.

Just when you thought it couldn't get any better…it does. So we have Jesus, seated at the right hand of God, interceding, pleading for us. We have the Spirit of God who is our advocate. And to top it all off…we have the promise of the Father that says, "The LORD himself goes before you and will be with you; he will never leave you nor forsake you. Do not be afraid; do not be discouraged." (Deuteronomy 31:8). We have God the Father; God the Son (Jesus); and God the Holy Spirit all in our corner. Not one, not two, but ALL THREE are with us.

So let's look back to the opening statement. You're never alone. We need to see that for what it is – a lie from the devil. That's his main tactic. He wants to confuse us; to convince us that we're all alone in what we're facing. While it may feel, at times, like you're alone–nothing could be further from the truth. The ones in our corner are always there.

DAY 38

"See, I am doing a new thing! Now it springs up; do you not perceive it? I am making a way in the wilderness and streams in the wasteland. (Isaiah 43:19)" A new life. Something different and refreshing. A change of pace. Each one of these phrases describes the feeling when we obtain something or experience something new in life. New is good. It's exciting…like the anticipation of a child tearing into gifts on Christmas day. We look forward to new things. They're longed for in our culture more than most anything else. Some people will do almost anything to get these new things. Anything except wait that is. My son — like most teenagers — has a perpetual problem. He hates to wait for things. He wants it and he wants it NOW! The phrase 'Good things come to those who wait' is meaningless in his life. He hates waiting. I can't say that I blame him. He sort of inherits that from his dad (having sheepishly typed that last sentence).

Waiting on things can be a good thing. If we didn't wait for the bread to rise the dough wouldn't bake properly. If we didn't wait for the fruit to ripen it would be bitter rather than sweet. There are so many things that are better when we wait for them! We wait for flowers, grass, and trees to grow in order to experience their full beauty.

So what does this have to do with the verse in Isaiah? A lot actually. We get tired of waiting for God to do something because we're not looking to see the new things He's bring about in us. We adopt the 15-year-old mentality that God has to do something NOW. And if He doesn't we fold our arms, stomp our feet, and whine like a 5-year-old. It's ok to admit that. I am. Yes…I have been a selfish 5-year-old with God.

If you've never been in the middle of the wilderness or the desert then count yourself lucky. If you want to experience it just drive through the Mojave Desert in California. There's nothing there. When you're in the middle of those places it can be difficult to focus on anything but the vastness of the wilderness you're in. Watching the road in front of you is difficult. It seems like you're just another grain of sand among the millions (more likely billions) out there. You begin to anticipate something — anything — that will change the landscape. It's even possible for your mind to conjure up things that you think you may see. And then the most beautiful thing you've ever seen shows up on the side of the road. It's an ugly sign that tells how many miles to the next town.

Life can be just like driving through a desert or wilderness. We get tired of waiting for the new thing to come. We're tired of the scenery and the journey. We would rather be on any other road but that one. But if we change roads in the middle of the wilderness all it does is get us lost. God says that there are pointers to the 'new things' He's bringing. He leaves markers that reveal you're on the right road — like the verse above. There can be an encouraging word from a friend that boosts your resolve to keep going. There's the sermon from a pastor that renews and refreshes the journey you're on. He lovingly tells us that new things are on their way…we just have to stay on the road that we're traveling. Anything that God has us wait for is definitely worth it.

DAY 39

As I drove home one evening from church I was thinking about what could be written that would inspire and encourage people. I began thinking about all the stuff that was going on and realized that life is pretty good. There are struggles and concerns but nothing that is really out of the ordinary for daily life. In thinking about this I was almost disappointed that there wasn't some struggle that I could glean a bit of spiritual wisdom from to pass on to anyone that needed it.

While rolling this over in my mind I could sense God touching my heart and mind. It was as if He was saying, "Just enjoy it." And then I realized that I didn't need some great struggle in order to see the goodness of God. It was (and still is) all around me all the time. We tend to see it more when we're shown some great revelation or when God provides in a spectacular way.

But what about the times when it's good? Life is moving along and we don't really need something specific from God. The car is working, the bills are paid, and our job is going well. All these things deserve recognition too. You see, for most of us we tend to seek

God when life is difficult. But when it's going good…we coast along. We enjoy the sunshine and roses. We skip along whistling a tune to ourselves and enjoy it. We ask for help with the clouds but enjoy the silver linings without God.

We can't, however, forget that God is working in the great times as well. David wrote about it in the Psalms. It's probably the most well-known one that he penned. "The Lord is my shepherd, I lack nothing. He makes me lie down in green pastures, he leads me beside quiet waters, he refreshes my soul. (Psalm 23:1-3)" We can't deny the working of God in our life when it's going good. In fact we need to do the exact opposite. In the times of refreshing and restoration we need to shout about the goodness of God all that much more.

In these verses David paints a picture of the ever vigilant shepherd taking care of his sheep. Everything that they need is provided by him. Rest, restoration, provision, and refreshment are all given in the required measurements to provide exactly what is needed when it is needed.

All too often we look at the struggles in life and fail to see the green pastures that he brings us to. I'm making an effort to look at the great times and acknowledge that they come from God. I think it's the least that I can do for all He has done (and continues to do) for me. As for this time…I'm lying in green pastures and I'm thanking God for leading me to it and allowing me the time of refreshing. At any moment it can change…but I'm enjoying it right now. Thanks God.

DAY 40

Psalm 23:4 is one of my favorite verses in the Bible (I have a lot of favorites). It reads: "Even though I walk through the darkest valley, I will fear no evil, for you are with me; your rod and your staff, they comfort me." Just recently I have had occasion to reflect on this verse. There have been some dark times in life. We all face them at one point or another. I find David's statement interesting in this verse though. He says, "I will fear no evil…" He makes a choice. He chooses to start fear in the face and say, "I won't listen to you."

Choices are interesting things. Some of us make them without regard to the consequences. Some make them based on circumstances. Some make them based on research. David didn't do any of these things. He was, most likely, faced with insurmountable odds (as he was much of his life). Yet he made a choice to not fear the evil that came against him. Why do you think that is? David's answer, "…for you are with me…"

David knew that no matter what came his way God was with

him. He had heard the stories of Israel's deliverance from Egypt. He knew the things that God had told them when faced with an impossible situation. God said, "The Lord will fight for you; you need only to be still." David also had personal experience with God's protection and deliverance. He said as much when standing before King Saul. "The Lord who rescued me from the paw of the lion and the paw of the bear will rescue me from the hand of this Philistine (1 Samuel 17:37)." And God did just what David expected.

When fear whispers in our ear that it's hopeless we have to choose not to listen. Instead we need to reflect on the times that God has been with us. Ponder the provision of God. Remember the revelation of God. Hold tight to the healing and comfort of God. In the darkest valley...those things will remind us that God is there.

Another reason that David could make the choice he did is because of this phrase, "...your rod and your staff, they comfort me." As a shepherd David understood the significance of what he was saying. The rod and staff were tools that the shepherd would use to protect, guide, and direct the sheep through anything that came along. God, as David's shepherd, could guide him through any circumstance or situation that arose. The thing I find comforting in all this is if God did that for David...He will for me too. And you as well. So that brings us to a choice. What will you choose? Fear or no fear?

DO YOU KNOW JESUS?

J esus is arguably the most influential person in human history. The Bible teaches, though, that he was more than that. The book of Isaiah prophesied His arrival more than 700 years before it happened. So what is knowing Jesus all about? We've heard terms like grace, mercy, and forgiveness of sins. But what do they really mean?

Everyone on the planet has one thing in common. This commonality doesn't depend on language, race, color, creed, gender, or anything else we can think of. "for all have sinned and fall short of the glory of God, (Romans 3:23)" Yes — it's true — you, me, the U.S. President, and the Pope have all sinned. No one escapes this. It is a reality.

Our sin — whether consciously or unconsciously committed — separates us from a God that desperately loves us. He loves us so much that He made a way for us to connect with Him. That way is through His Son, Jesus.

- ...I am the way and the truth and the life. No one comes to the Father except through me. (John 14:6)
- For God so loved the world that he gave his one and only

Son, that whoever believes in him shall not perish but have eternal life. (John 3:16)

"But I'm a good person! I haven't done anything remotely wrong." Well...the Bible deals with that too.

- All of us have become like one who is unclean, and all our righteous acts are like filthy rags; we all shrivel up like a leaf, and like the wind our sins sweep us away. (Isaiah 64:6)

- For it is by grace you have been saved, through faith—and this is not from yourselves, it is the gift of God— not by works, so that no one can boast. (Ephesians 2:8-9)

In order to connect with God our sins must be paid for. Every one of us has to pay God's price for our sins. And the price is really steep.

- For the wages of sin is death...(Romans 6:23)

- In fact, the law requires that nearly everything be cleansed with blood, and without the shedding of blood there is no forgiveness. (Hebrews 9:22)

But there is another way. God provided a way for us to connect with Him and have the price for our sins paid for by another. Remember the verses above about God giving His Son? Well...that was Jesus. And He actually paid the price for us. All we have to do is accept this gift. "...but the gift of God is eternal life in Christ Jesus our Lord. (Romans 6:23)" It really is that easy. And the cool thing is that you don't have to come with all the answers. All you have to do is believe. The Bible calls it 'being saved'.

- If we confess our sins, he is faithful and just and will forgive us our sins and purify us from all unrighteousness. (1 John 1:9)

- If you declare with your mouth, "Jesus is Lord," and believe in your heart that God raised him from the dead, you will be saved. (Romans 10:9)

That's really all it takes. And when you do that...God promises that your sins are paid for. How? Jesus died for them. He paid the price for you, me, and every other person on the planet. It only takes one simple sincere prayer to be sure that you know Jesus and that your sins (the things that separate you from God) are forgiven. Simply say this prayer loud enough for yourself to hear it — believing that God heard you — and He does the rest.

Dear Jesus,

Thank You for loving me. Thank You for reaching out to me. And today, Jesus, I'm reaching back. I understand that I am a sinner and separated from You. I am asking for forgiveness of those sins and for You to be my sin-bearer. Thank You for paying the price for me. And now I boldly say, with my new faith, I am forgiven...born again...saved. And I'll never, never, never be the same again. In Jesus' name, Amen.

Congratulations! Now you know Jesus. If you have prayed that prayer and accepted Jesus into your life...please tell someone so they can celebrate with you. I recommend that you find a good, Bible-believing and Bible-teaching church to attend so you can learn more about life in Christ. Finally, let me be the first to welcome you into God's family.

ABOUT THE AUTHOR

Jeffrey Wilson is an Ordained Minister and has served in various pastoral positions for the past 20 years. His most recent was as senior pastor of Springs in the Desert Church in Indio, CA. He is the author of Drawing From The Well that has been read in over 50 countries.
(http://drawingfromthewell.wordpress.com) He recently relocated to Southeast Missouri where he feels that God is moving him into another dimension of ministry. He lives there with his wife, Julee, and their three children, Erik, Matthew, and Emma. His deepest desire is to share the Word of God with as many people as he can.

www.ingramcontent.com/pod-product-compliance
Lightning Source LLC
Chambersburg PA
CBHW060943040426
42445CB00011B/975